"Where did you come from,
Baby dear?
Out of the everywhere,
Into here."

—George MacDonald

Dear Friends,

The birth of a child is one of the most profound experiences we can ever have. And it is just the beginning. From the moment the little guest arrives, he brings and shares with us the light and purity of the Creator. As we nurture him and watch him grow and blossom, we may see again the wonder of this mysterious world through innocent eyes.

Alas, our memories are such unreliable witnesses. This book is for you to write down what you can, when you can—and you will be creating a keepsake you and your child will treasure. We hope you enjoy using this book as much as we enjoyed making it.

Michael & Sally Green
Philadelphia, 1981

First Days on the Planet Earth

Affix first pictures of Baby here—note when taken, where & by whom; how many hours, days, weeks old was Baby?

First Imprints & Bonding

Getting to know each other

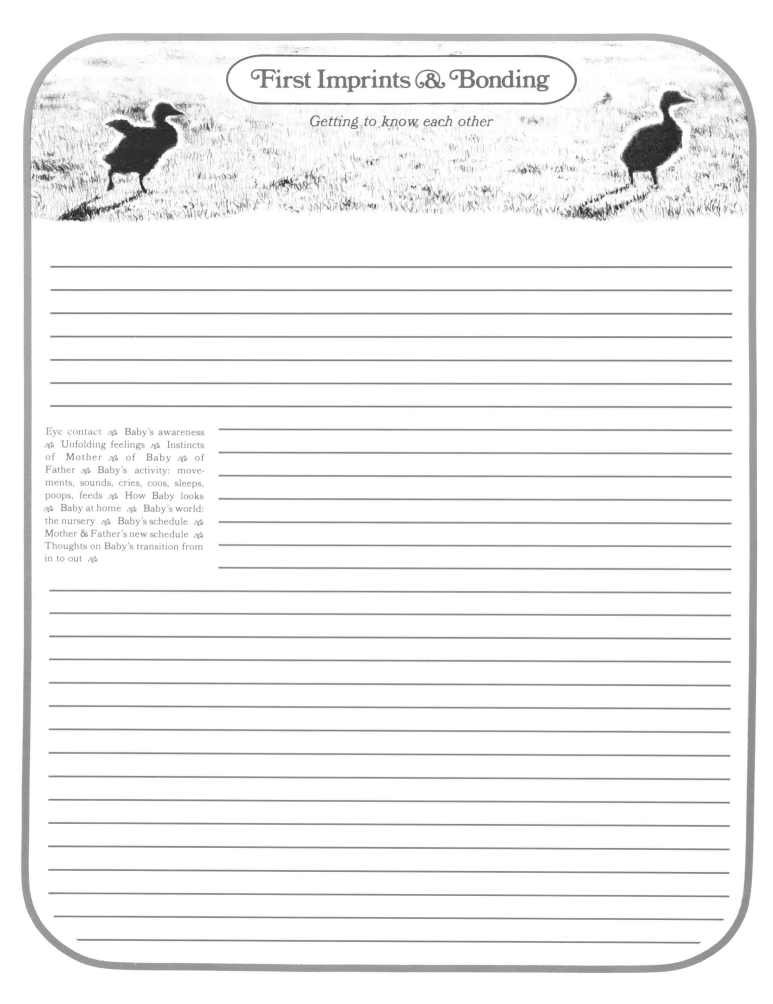

Eye contact ❧ Baby's awareness ❧ Unfolding feelings ❧ Instincts of Mother ❧ of Baby ❧ of Father ❧ Baby's activity: movements, sounds, cries, coos, sleeps, poops, feeds ❧ How Baby looks ❧ Baby at home ❧ Baby's world: the nursery ❧ Baby's schedule ❧ Mother & Father's new schedule ❧ Thoughts on Baby's transition from in to out ❧

First Imprints & Bonding

Visitor's Log

Sharing the joy

Who came ❧ When ❧ Their impressions ❧ Comments, advice, suggestions, warnings from the experts ❧ Gifts for Baby ❧ For Mother ❧ Flowers ❧ Signatures ❧ Pictures of Baby & admirers ❧

Visitor's Log

Elsewhere in the World

A sampler of the day's events

The day's headlines ❧ Weather ❧ Politics ❧ Presidents ❧ Kings & queens ❧ Big events ❧ Scientific achievements & advances ❧ Philosophy ❧ Humor ❧ Quote for the day ❧ Entertainment ❧ Movies ❧ Books ❧ Television ❧ Theater ❧ Music ❧ Dance ❧ Art ❧ Sports ❧ Fashion ❧ Technology ❧ Local news ❧ Costs, prices, salaries ❧ Jobs & occupations ❧ Cars ❧ Notable names ❧ Faces ❧ Feelings ❧ Predictions & forecasts ❧

Elsewhere in the World

Elsewhere in the World

Elsewhere in the World

...And in the Heavens

*For your information or amusement,
record the exact moment of birth*

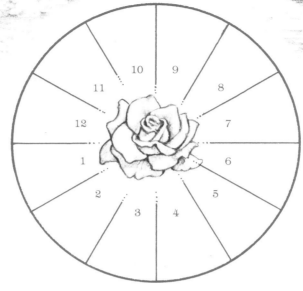

Date _____

Time _____

Place _____

Longitude _____

Latitude _____

Earth _____

Air _____

Fire _____

Water _____

☉ **Sun sign** _____

☽ **Moon sign** _____

⚹ **Rising sign** _____

☿ Mercury _____

♀ Venus _____

♂ Mars _____

♃ Jupiter _____

♄ Saturn _____

♅ Uranus _____

♆ Neptune _____

♇ Pluto _____

Mid-Heaven _____

Interpretation _____

_____

_____

_____

_____

_____

_____

_____

_____

_____

_____

_____

_____

_____

_____

The Family Chronicles

Affix a picture of the whole family.
You might want to put initials of
Baby's parents in the heart on the
tree trunk.

D. P.
+
C. L.

Loughlin
mother's family name

Pimental
father's family name

Grandparents

Grandfather's picture, with short history below. Include full name, date & place of birth.

Grandmother's picture, with short history below. Include full name, date & place of birth.

Grandparents

Father's side

Grandfather's picture, with short history below. Include full name, date & place of birth.

Grandmother's picture, with short history below. Include full name, date & place of birth.

Mother

Her story

Affix picture, & write short history
below.

Father

His story

Affix picture, & write short history
below.

Roots & Flowers

Cut out circular picture of Baby & affix here.

Other flowers are for brothers, sisters, or whomever. Space next to Mother & Father are for aunts, uncles, cousins, or to diagram more complex relationships involving previous marriages.

Grandfather

Grandmother

Father

Mother

Grandfather

Grandmother

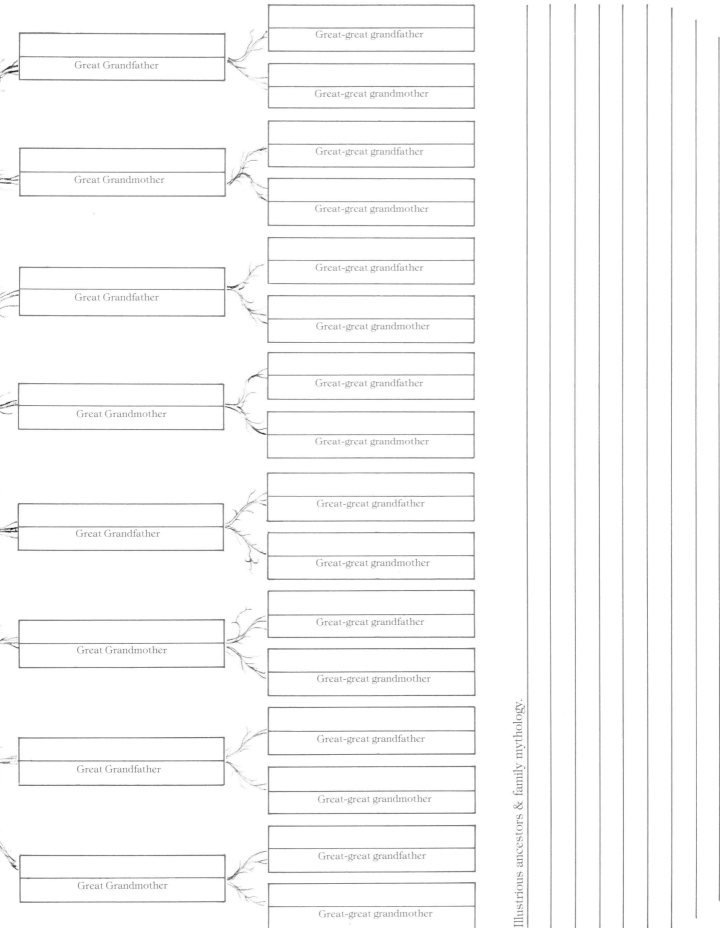

| Great Grandfather |
| Great-great grandfather |
| Great-great grandmother |

| Great Grandmother |
| Great-great grandfather |
| Great-great grandmother |

| Great Grandfather |
| Great-great grandfather |
| Great-great grandmother |

| Great Grandmother |
| Great-great grandfather |
| Great-great grandmother |

| Great Grandfather |
| Great-great grandfather |
| Great-great grandmother |

| Great Grandmother |
| Great-great grandfather |
| Great-great grandmother |

| Great Grandfather |
| Great-great grandfather |
| Great-great grandmother |

| Great Grandmother |
| Great-great grandfather |
| Great-great grandmother |

Illustrious ancestors & family mythology.

The Clan

A family reunion

Diagram all brothers, sisters, cousins & second cousins, rich uncles, favorite aunts, eccentric grandfathers—every relative you can think of.

The Care & Feeding of Baby

Growing Up

For good measure

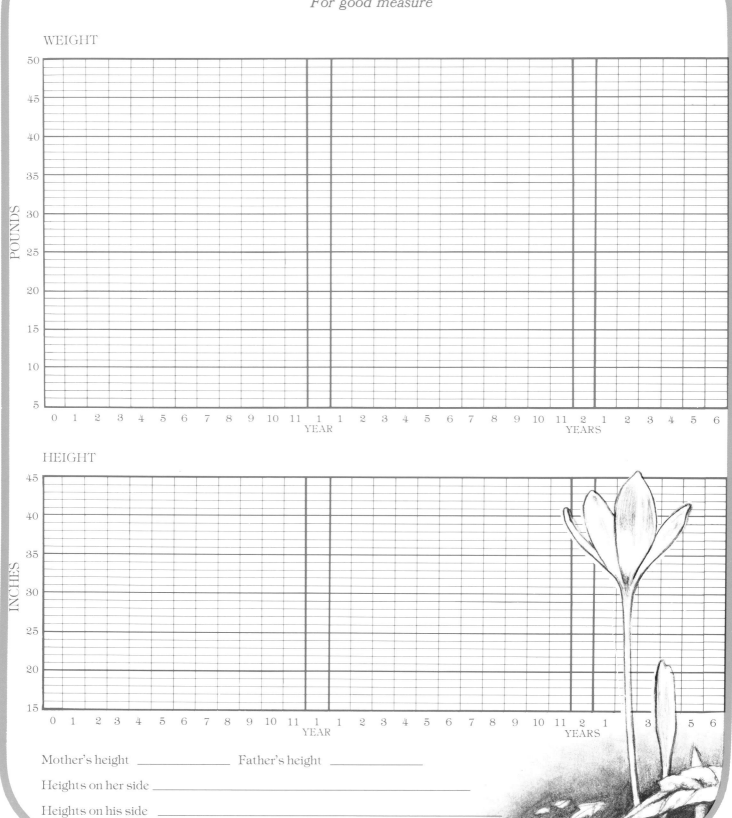

WEIGHT

POUNDS

50
45
40
35
30
25
20
15
10
5

0 1 2 3 4 5 6 7 8 9 10 11 1 1 2 3 4 5 6 7 8 9 10 11 2 1 2 3 4 5 6
YEAR   YEARS

HEIGHT

INCHES

45
40
35
30
25
20
15

0 1 2 3 4 5 6 7 8 9 10 11 1 1 2 3 4 5 6 7 8 9 10 11 2 1 3   5 6
YEAR   YEARS

Mother's height _____ Father's height _____

Heights on her side _____

Heights on his side _____

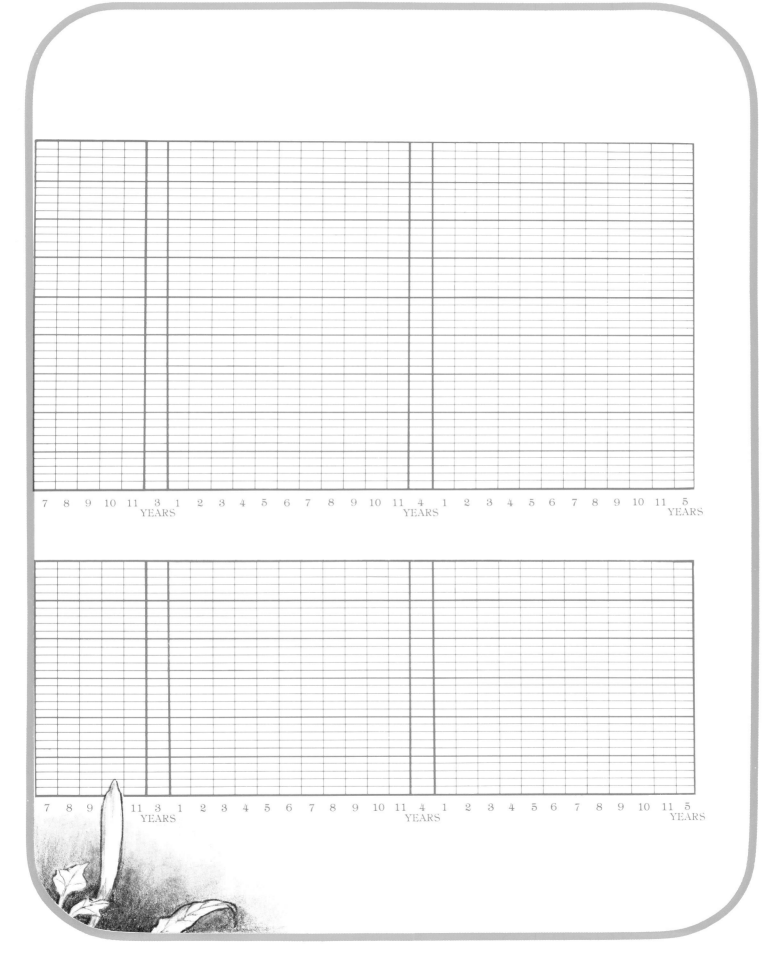

7 8 9 10 11 3 1 2 3 4 5 6 7 8 9 10 11 4 1 2 3 4 5 6 7 8 9 10 11 5
YEARS   YEARS   YEARS

7 8 9   11 3 1 2 3 4 5 6 7 8 9 10 11 4 1 2 3 4 5 6 7 8 9 10 11 5
YEARS   YEARS   YEARS

Visits to the Doctor

Check ups, tune-ups & fix-ups

Doctor _Aquavella_ Date _11|9|90_ Age _i week_ Weight _7 lbs 10 oz_ Height _Same_

Questions for Doctor _____

Doctor's comments & recommendations _____

_____

Doctor _Katzen_ Date _11|13|90_ Age _11 days_ Weight _____ Height _____

Questions for Doctor _First cast change. How long for cast,_

Doctor's comments & recommendations _Maybe 8 weeks for cast. Exercises for (L) foot_

_____

Doctor _____ Date _____ Age _____ Weight _____ Height _____

Questions for Doctor _____

Doctor's comments & recommendations _____

_____

Doctor _____ Date _____ Age _____ Weight _____ Height _____

Questions for Doctor _____

Doctor's comments & recommendations _____

_____

Doctor _____ Date _____ Age _____ Weight _____ Height _____

Questions for Doctor _____

Doctor's comments & recommendations _____

_____

Doctor _____ Date _____ Age _____ Weight _____ Height _____

Questions for Doctor _____

Doctor's comments & recommendations _____

_____

Visits to the Doctor

Doctor _____ Date _____ Age _____ Weight _____ Height _____

Questions for Doctor _____

Doctor's comments & recommendations _____

_____

Doctor _____ Date _____ Age _____ Weight _____ Height _____

Questions for Doctor _____

Doctor's comments & recommendations _____

_____

Doctor _____ Date _____ Age _____ Weight _____ Height _____

Questions for Doctor _____

Doctor's comments & recommendations _____

_____

Visits to the Doctor

Doctor _____ Date _____ Age _____ Weight _____ Height _____

Questions for Doctor _____

Doctor's comments & recommendations _____

_____

Doctor _____ Date _____ Age _____ Weight _____ Height _____

Questions for Doctor _____

Doctor's comments & recommendations _____

_____

Doctor _____ Date _____ Age _____ Weight _____ Height _____

Questions for Doctor _____

Doctor's comments & recommendations _____

_____

Doctor _____ Date _____ Age _____ Weight _____ Height _____

Questions for Doctor _____

Doctor's comments & recommendations _____

_____

Doctor _____ Date _____ Age _____ Weight _____ Height _____

Questions for Doctor _____

Doctor's comments & recommendations _____

_____

Doctor _____ Date _____ Age _____ Weight _____ Height _____

Questions for Doctor _____

Doctor's comments & recommendations _____

_____

Health History

Bumps, bruises, coughs, colds & assorted maladies

Problem	Date	Age	Treatment & Comments

Immunization Record

The preventive maintenance plan

Age **10 weeks** Innoculation **DPT, Hib, OPV** Date **1/11/91** Doctor **aquavella**
Reaction & Comments **none**

Age **4 months** Innoculation **DPT, Hib, OPV** Date **3/8/91** Doctor **aquavella**
Reaction & Comments **none**

Age **6 months** Innoculation **DPT, Hib, OPV** Date **5/3/91** Doctor
Reaction & Comments

Age_____ Innoculation_____ Date_____ Doctor_____
Reaction & Comments _____

Age_____ Innoculation_____ Date_____ Doctor_____
Reaction & Comments _____

Age_____ Innoculation_____ Date_____ Doctor_____
Reaction & Comments _____

Age_____ Innoculation_____ Date_____ Doctor_____
Reaction & Comments _____

Little Teeth

Starring, in order of their appearance . . .

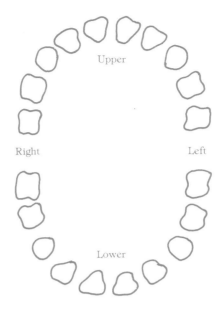

Upper

Right

Left

Lower

Fill in date as each tooth appears.

Teething problems & solutions.

Dentist_____Date_____Age_____Comments_____

_____

Dentist_____Date_____Age_____Comments_____

_____

Dentist_____Date_____Age_____Comments_____

_____

Dentist_____Date_____Age_____Comments_____

_____

Dentist_____Date_____Age_____Comments_____

_____

Eating & Sleeping & Eating & Sleeping

Finding the basic rhythms

How Baby takes to first feeding ❧ Breast or bottle ❧ Type of formula ❧ Schedule ❧ Or lack of ❧ Baby's feeding style ❧ Favorite position ❧ Problems with breast feeding/bottle feeding ❧ Introducing solid foods ❧ Feeding games played with Baby ❧ Weaning Baby ❧ Vitamins ❧ Indigestion —diarrhea, constipation, allergies, colic ❧ Cures ❧ Baby's sleep schedule ❧ How it evolves ❧ Favorite lullabies ❧ The night shift ❧

The Baby's Journal

Milestones

Firsts, lasts, & rites of passage

Age & Remarks

Around 8 weeks. Great feeling! _____ Recognizes & responds to Mother

1|1|91 Happy New Year Dad! _____ Recognizes & responds to Father

_____ Follows a moving object with eyes

We think he started smiling during first few weeks, could have been gas. definite smiles since 6 weeks — Smiles

Since about 4 weeks _____ Holds head up while prone

Since about 4-6 weeks _____ Puts hands to mouth

_____ First outings

10 weeks able to hold rattle _____ Holds an object

Since about 7-8 weeks, so cute, so happy _____ Laughs aloud

_____ Makes sounds to show displeasure

4 1/2 mos _____ Plays with own hands and feet

_____ Kicks & uses feet to push

1|4|91 _____ Sleeps through the night

Four months, took a few weeks to get used to the idea, first cereal 4 3/4 mos. Eats solid food

3|10 rolls from tummy to back + back to tummy _____ Rolls over

December 17th → _____ Reaches for objects

2|11|91 _____ Sits with support

5|15 6 mos. _____ Sits unaided

8|2|91 nine mos bottom right _____ First tooth

seven mos - cheerios! _____ Finger foods

_____ Babbles

April 25th c help _____ Drinks from a cup

April 18 _____ Holds a spoon

June 1st - 7 mos _____ Creeps

July 1st - eight mos _____ Crawls

July 15th 8 1/2 mos _____ Pulls up to stand

_____ Fully weaned

8 1/2 mos _____ Throws & drops objects

a mos _____ Responds to a mirror

"Da Da" _____ First word

September 17th 10 1/2 mos. _____ First step

Milestones

Age & Remarks

_____ First haircut

_____ Climbs stairs

_____ Stands alone

_____ Walks

_____ First shoes

_____ Names for Mother and Father

_____ Toilet training started

_____ Toilet training completed

_____ Learns to count

_____ Says own name

_____ First friends

_____ First day at nursery school

_____

_____

_____

_____

_____

_____

_____

_____

_____

_____

_____

_____

_____

_____

_____

_____

The Journal

Onward!

_____
_____
_____
_____

Every child unfolds at his or her own rate, & every parent will write a different kind of account. Therefore, the rest of the journal is open with this general list of ideas to draw from. Remember, many things which seem commonplace or insignificant now, may be fascinating pieces of information in the future. When in doubt, write!

How we want to raise Baby ❧ Hopes & plans & theories on parenting & how they are working out ❧ Traits & habits we hope Baby inherits ❧ Ones we hope Baby doesn't ❧ Books read ❧ Rites of passage—naming Baby, circumcision, baptism, godparents ❧ First communications with Baby—how he responds to touch, looks, sounds, lights, colors, voices, music ❧ What we are learning from Baby ❧ Caring for Baby ❧ Baby's outings ❧ Baby's reactions ❧ Baby's clothes—favorites of Baby ❧ Favorites of Mother & Father ❧ Baby's delights—things & people Baby likes ❧ Secret techniques for cheering Baby up ❧ Baby's fears—things & people ❧ Baby gets it together—raises head, rolls over, sits up, creeps, crawls, & cruises ❧ Baby becomes a biped

The Journal

ஃ Mother & Father rearrange the house ஃ Baby's temperament, habits, mannerisms ஃ Baby's favorite toy or security blanket ஃ Baby's problems—sleeping, eating, digesting ஃ Silly Baby ஃ Baby's tricks ஃ Getting frustrated with Baby ஃ Getting over it ஃ Baby's favorite songs & stories & lullabies ஃ Toilet training Baby ஃ Baby's friends ஃ Baby learns it's a hard world ஃ First sentence ஃ The wit & wisdom of Baby ஃ Baby as a little person ஃ Glimpses of the future person—tendencies & talents ஃ The world of make believe ஃ A child's fears ஃ A child away from home ஃ At school ஃ New friends ஃ New interests ஃ New problems ஃ A child's drawings ஃ Scribblings ஃ A child's insights ஃ A child on the rampage ஃ A child's new responsibilities ஃ Girls will be girls & boys will be boys & vice versa ஃ Trikes & bikes & training wheels ஃ A child's questions ஃ A child's instinct ஃ

The Journal

The Journal

The Journal

The Journal

The Journal

The Journal

The Journal

The Journal

The Journal

The Journal

The Journal

The Journal

The Journal

The Journal

The Journal

The Archives

Records, documents & keepsakes

The Journal

The Archives

Records, documents & keepsakes

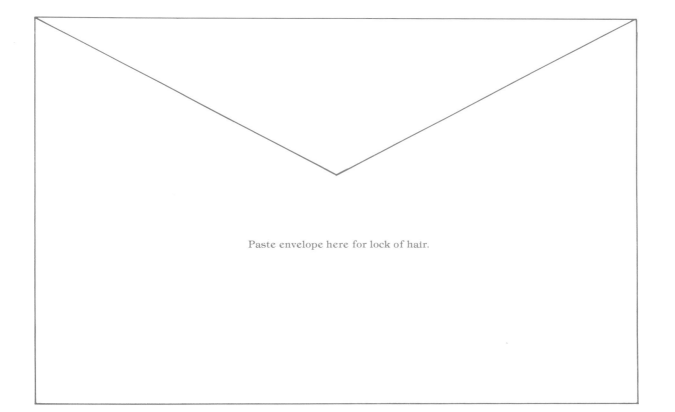

Paste envelope here for lock of hair.

To Be Continued . . .